Looking for Cover

DATE DUE

Demco, Inc. 38-293

MAR 2 3 2009

Looking for Cover

POEMS BY MARIA FAMÀ

BORDIGHERA PRESS

Library of Congress Control Number: 2007926838

© 2007 by Maria Famà
Cover photograph, "Doorway," © Russ R. Fama

Printed in the United States.

Published by
BORDIGHERA PRESS
John D. Calandra Italian American Institute
25 West 43rd Street, 17th Floor
New York, NY 10036

VIA Folios 45
ISBN 1-884419-85-2

Grateful acknowledgment is made to the editors
of the following publications where some
of these poems first appeared:

*American Writing; Bogg; Breaking Open; Futureworks; Hey!; Identity
Lessons; La Bella Figura; Labyrinth; Liberty Hill Poetry Review; Paterson
Literary Review; Pearl; Phati'tude; Philadelphia Poets; Seven Arts
Magazine; Sinister Wisdom; Sweet Lemons; VIA: Voices in Italian
Americana;* and *The Writer.*

The following poems have been awarded as follows:

"My Mother's Prayer List," The Amy Tritsch Needle Award for Poetry, 2006
"Table Back," Aniello Lauri Award for Creative Writing, 2005
"Valentine Teen Dance at the Aquarama," Editor's Choice,
    Paterson Literary Review, 2003
"Pasta e Piselli," "Ghazal #1," and "Pear Trees," Aniello Lauri Award for
    Creative Writing, 2002
"6:35 A.M.," Finalist, Allen Ginsberg Poetry Awards, 1998
"Laura," Honorable Mention, Allen Ginsberg Poetry Awards, 1995
"Nonna Mattia," Honorable Mention, Allen Ginsberg Poetry Awards, 1994

*This book is dedicated to my parents, grandparents, and Anita,
who all inspired me in life and continue to inspire me
from the spirit world.*

CONTENTS

PART THREE

SPIRIT WORLD

PART FOUR

UNDER THE TENT
PERFORMANCE POEMS

PART ONE

SHIELDS AND SHELTER

CONVERSATION WITH MARY BUCCI BUSH

They are in the kitchen
those shades of the grandfathers
   sitting at our sides
   at the table

we are two friends
writers   women
   talking
about our grandfathers
who learned to read by oil lamp and candlelight
each packed a favorite book
for the journey across the sea
her grandfather carried THE ARABIAN NIGHTS
mine THE BRIDGE OF SIGHS

They are in the kitchen
those shades of the grandmothers
   standing over our shoulders
   by the stove
as we stir the soup, cut the bread
tell each other about
my only child grandmother, sent to school
by her illiterate wet nurse mother,
who sold a pair of earrings so her son
could study the trumpet
my father traveled Sicily in a symphonic band
   because of her

Mary speaks to me of her grandmother
who urged her daughter
to go to school, become a teacher
buy a car
be the first Italian, let alone a woman,
to drive a car in a little New York state town

We talk over the pasta and the insalata mista
the shades of the aunts and uncles
   stand by the door
   attentive that we speak their stories
the Aunt who taught Math
the Aunt who learned to read and write
in one year from an old, neighbor lady
the Uncle who left the coalmines
injured and cursing Christ to become a master chef
The shades of poetry reciting onion farmers
the shades of opera singing coalminers
squeeze into the kitchen
as we chat, sharing what we know
   of their stories
the snatches we heard growing up
   around the kitchen table
     eating pasta e piselli, fagioli,
     pastina in brodo, ceci, pesce spada
     pane and biscotti

The shades of the relatives
and the comari and compari
   crowd us at the table
they want us to get it right

4

They whisper for us to drink our wine
   sip our espresso and remember
when we speak of them

that their struggle for bread was fierce
they wept because they could not afford school or books
music filled their lives
prayers, proverbs, memorized poems comforted them

The shades are with us
around the table
they want us to tell
   of their great desire to learn
   of their great desire to better their lives.

TABLE BACK

My great-grandfather's father, Giuseppe Bongiovanni,
bent at a right angle from arthritis,
joked that his family could place their bread and olives
upon his back as they farmed the hot Sicilian fields

When my great-grandfather, Pietro, returned from America
in a suit with bowler hat and shiny black shoes
he rushed to the mountainside plot
where his father was bent over the land

Giuseppe saw only creased black pants and expensive shoes
   coming toward him
"Pa!" called Pietro
"Vossia," answered Giuseppe addressing him formally
   with great deference
"Pa, sugnu yo, to' figghiu!"
Giuseppe lifted his head
looked into Pietro's ruddy face with the waxed mustache
He recognized his son's sea-blue eyes
   under a rich man's hat
"Figghiu miu," he smiled
Pietro bent down to kiss Giuseppe's grizzled cheeks

They walked slowly home
Pietro holding the calloused hand
of his table backed father.

translation:
"Vossia"= Your Excellency; "Pa, sugnu yo, to' figghiu!"= Pa, it's me, your son! "Figghiu miu"=My son

PEAR TREES

My father, Nonno Saro's namesake,
pointed to the lush, green pear trees
   on a Sicilian hillside
told me how my great grandfather
planted them years ago
when the land was worked, but not owned,
   by our family

Nonno Saro had sweated hard in the sun
planting the saplings he nurtured
almost tasting the sweet pears
he'd someday pick for his family

My father said
we gave most everything to the Duke
   who owned the land
we kept just a little for ourselves
one day an overseer for the Duke rode by
   high up on horseback
he told Nonno Saro
"Pull up those pear saplings
the Duke wants only wine this year
plant grape vines there!"

Nonno Saro was so furious
he addressed the overseer as "tu"
the familiar you, a terrible insult:
"You, get down off that horse
you pull the saplings up yourself!"

Nonno Saro had decided to kill the overseer
he'd hit him with a shovel as he dismounted
Nonno Saro wanted the overseer dead at his feet
His wife tugged his arm,"Calm down, let's go home"

Nonno Saro's anger boiled
he pushed his wife aside
ran toward the overseer
held his shovel high, ready to strike
the horse reared up
fear crossed the overseer's face
he reined in the horse, rode away

My father said Nonno Saro made peace the next day
brought a basket of fresh eggs to the overseer

with pride and tenderness
my father pointed to the green hill
"The pear trees are still there."

TABLECLOTH

Nonna Angela speaks to me in May

She returns with May roses
She comes with May sunshine

My great-great grandmother speaks to me in May

>   when I cover the dining room table
>   with the tablecloth she wove
>   over one hundred years ago
>   I set a vase on the dazzling center
>   and a voice scented with roses
>   whispers into a shaft of sun.

Nonna Angela grew cotton from a seed
She spun and wove the fabric on a rickety loom
She washed and rinsed it in a mountain stream

Nonna Angela pounded the cloth on rocks
and let the hot Sicilian sun bleach
the tablecloth a gleaming white
for her daughter's wedding day.

Nonna Angela speaks to me in May

>   I know her still young and twice-widowed
>   her sun-struck face hopeful
>   for five children to find a good life.

Nonna Angela embroidered with field-roughened hands
tiny May flowers, pea pods and blossoms
on the tablecloth's borders
long-life and fertility, embroidered wishes,
for her oldest girl.

> The tablecloth has come down to me
> over a century of Mays and mothers
> across an ocean
> to grace my city table every Spring

Nonna Angela speaks to me in May
I answer in gratitude
for her long-ago labor of love
                        and of hope

NONNA MATTIA

Nonna Mattia,

great grandmother

large and generous

I ask for your strength

I found your hand made apron

in an old chest of drawers
I shook it out
neat cross hatched stitches of repairs
rise like sailboats
across the billowing white

I think of the storms
of your ocean crossings
first with your new husband
traveling from sun baked mountains
to an Ohio mining town
then, having lost your first child
you sailed alone and pregnant
to deliver your second in Sicily

with your mother at your side

You crossed again the ocean expanse
with a year old daughter

returning to your husband's American home

I wrap the apron around me twice
and there is room left over
as I look for cover
in your largeness of body and heart

You wore this apron in Ohio
across Pennsylvania   into Philadelphia
in Jersey fields as you picked crops
in the city as you prepared meals
scrubbed laundry   took in boarders

nursed the sick and dying

Nonna Mattia,

I remember you elderly and brave
caring for me with smiles and laughter
your coal black eyes watching the world
as you sang in clear Sicilian cadence

Nonna Mattia,

I wrap the apron around me twice
as I look for cover in your
largeness of body and heart

Grant me a portion of your
robustness of spirit, great grandmother

Let this apron be my shield
Let this apron transfer your strong faith
your compassion and your courage
to me, your great granddaughter.

THE BANANAS

In early 1939
my father rode the train to Palermo to get his documents
for his immigration to America
where he'd join his father and brother already there

Afterwards, with his documents in order,
sixteen year old Saro Famà strolled the Palermo streets
with a third class return ticket and a few coins in his pocket

Near the station, he eyed the bright yellow bananas
of a fruit vendor
he had never eaten a banana
he'd seen a straggly wild banana tree in a field
near his little Sicilian hometown of San Pier Niceto
but he had never seen such beautiful brilliant bananas
except in pictures of tropical isles

Even though in his family
they only ate fruit they grew themselves
he bought two bananas paying with all the money he had
he put the firm smooth-jacketed fruit
in his own jacket pocket

Saro boarded the crowded train home
sitting on the hard wooden seat
thinking of the banana surprise he'd give
his mother, grandfather, and little sister
the bananas smelled of leisure, of romance, of exotic lands
Saro wondered about the bananas in America

he guessed that they must be plentiful and cheap there
everything you ever wanted was in America he'd been told

The train rattled along the dream-like coast
the wintry sea dark and choppy
as my father dozed

When he awoke near his Milazzo stop
he realized that in his sleep he had slumped
against the wooden bench
crushing the bananas
which now were split and oozed their sweetly scented pulp
into his jacket pocket
getting the bananas together as best he could
disappointment around his heart
Saro made his way home where
he placed the damaged bananas on the table
apologizing for destroying their beauty in his sleep

Yet his mother, sister, and grandfather
smiled and shouted with delight
my grandmother carefully undid the bananas' sticky skins
she scraped every bit of banana onto a plate
she spooned equal shares of fruit for each of them

My father, his mother, his sister, and his grandfather
all ate the treat slowly
all savoring the exotic taste of the bananas
all dreaming of faraway lands of plenty, leisure, and romance.

PASTA E PISELLI: LUNCHTIME MEMORIES
of my Grandmother Maria Concetta Adamo Famà

Pasta e piselli   piselli e pasta
a simple lunch   poor people's feast

during the second world war
your Aunt Domenica and I were alone

        in Sicily

    the Germans in town
    the Americans advancing

your grandfather in New Jersey
an enemy land   no letters allowed
he'd sent for his sons just before the war
I knew my sons were fighting for the Americans

your aunt and I were alone
        and often hungry

Put the garlic and olive oil and some onions in the pan
    when they're golden throw in the peas
    fresh or frozen whatever you have
    add some water   let them cook
    throw in the basil, salt, pepper if you like
    a little parsley

the miseria got so bad
winters were the worse
all we had to eat were onions, olives
some dried fruit, a little wine
  forget about pasta
  hard then to even make bread
the grain was on the trains heading for Germany

I had no brothers, no sisters
  my parents were dead
all alone your aunt and I

once I heard there was contraband meat
I walked seven kilometers
to get a piece as big as a baby's fist
  for your aunt
she was thirteen, had to grow, had to develop

I roasted that tough little piece for her
  watched her eat
I ate a few olives, drank some wine
she wanted to give me some
No I said you're growing
  you need it
  I'm already grown
I never had much taste for meat
I never eat it now

So, now we put water on to boil
  for the pasta
check the peas, let them simmer
they smell good, no?

poor people's feast
pasta e piselli
piselli e pasta

Those days during the war
  the cat was eating soap
  she was so hungry
  not even enough birds or mice to eat
such miseria

I had a little money put aside
but I couldn't buy a thing
I went to buy grain once
the man said there was none
I noticed one speck of golden wheat
  on the floor
I covered it with my foot   stood there
  as people came in
  went away with hungry hearts
when no one else was there
  I said   Signore, you have grain
  I have a piece under my foot
He begged me not to report him to the fascists
  he gave me a small bag
  I never told
we had a little bread for awhile
I burned rags when I baked it so nobody knew

You can cut us some bread
  from this nice loaf
  the water is boiling

I put in the pasta
I like little shells, penne, fusilli
 but any pasta is good

When I came here to my husband's house
 in 1946
here was this stove
no more walking for wood
no more kindling a flame
just turn a knob, blue flame, a miracle

The Germans were finally chased out
one day we saw American soldiers
 riding into town
I cried to see that flag
carried by those rowdy young men
 that all the young women
 were kissing and cheering
I kept my daughter close
hid her as I did from the Germans
 but those boys could've been my sons
 riding in a jeep
 somewhere in the world

Let's take the pasta down
 we drain it
put the peas in with the pasta
mix it up good, put it in the dishes
grate the cheese over the pasta
 piselli e pasta
 pasta e piselli

Wash the cherries
we'll have fruit afterwards

we had our own cherry trees in Sicily
when we ate cherries in the summertime
 we got healthy

one day your aunt and I
went to pick our cherries
American soldiers sat in our trees
 eating cherries
your aunt was angry
 Chase them away, Mamma
I told her
 Let them eat   let them enjoy
 maybe somewhere my sons are hungry
 and there are cherry trees for them

The Madonna saved us all
 from the war

we have had our feast
pasta e piselli   piselli e pasta
 fruit, too

a simple lunch
poor people's feast.

CHOOSING

My grandmothers were born eight years apart
in a Sicilian farming village
at a time when food was precious
where there was often hunger
where the saying went, "Who does not eat dies."

My grandmothers died ten years apart
in the United States
Maria Concetta at 86 in 1986
Domenica at 88 in 1996
tired of life with all its struggles and pain
husbands long dead
children established in this new land
where food was plentiful
where everybody was on a diet

Maria Concetta liked the heat, Elvis, and Lawrence Welk
Domenica liked the cold,
Grand Opera, and Lawrence Welk
both had high blood pressure
both broke bones after bad falls
both were placed in rehab centers
where they refused to do physical therapy
refused to walk again
wanting their earthly lives to be over

In 1986, in the New Jersey nursing facility
Maria Concetta told children and grandchildren
"I want to die."

In 1996, in the Pennsylvania nursing facility
Domenica told children and grandchildren
"Let me die in peace."

Maria Concetta, who said,
"Too bad you can't walk yourself to the cemetery,"
thought she'd try to hurry herself along
Domenica, who said,
"Make sure I'm really dead before you bury me,"
told everybody she was "on the way out"
In 1986 and 1996 they refused to eat the institutional meals
their daughters brought
home-cooked meals they would not eat
their friends brought
home-cooked meals they would not eat

In 1986 Maria Concetta told her daughter,
"Bring me cannoli and wine."
For a month that's all she ate and drank
In 1996 Domenica told her daughters,
"Bring me hard boiled eggs and coffee."
For a month that's all she ate and drank

Then, Maria Concetta refused cannoli, only drinking wine
Then, Domenica refused
hard boiled eggs, only drinking coffee

In 1986 and 1996
their children and grandchildren begged them to eat
their comari begged them to eat
telling them they were wrong to choose to die

telling them they were making a sin
Maria Concetta said,
"I'll discuss it with God when I see him."
Domenica only shrugged.

In 1986, Maria Concetta stopped drinking her wine
In 1996, Domenica stopped drinking her coffee
In 1986, the doctors in New Jersey
asked her children to permit
a feeding tube for Maria Concetta
In 1996, the doctors in Pennsylvania
asked her children to permit a feeding tube for Domenica

In 1986 Maria Concetta's children bravely refused
loving their mother enough to honor her wish
In 1996 Domenica's children bravely refused
loving their mother enough to honor her wish

Maria Concetta in 1986   Domenica in 1996
My grandmothers died
at the time of their own choosing.

PART TWO

DOORWAYS AND CROSSROADS

I AM NOT WHITE

The dentist says my teeth tell of invasions
   mixed blood
the tale of a proud, mongrel people
  I am Sicilian
  I am not white
I will not check the box for white
  on any form

In Sicily
my ancestors recognized white
to be the color of sparkling linens
   towels, tablecloths, sheets
    the color of clouds, seafoam, and bones
not family faces with their
   African, Greek, Arabic, Norman casts

North Italians call us Africans
a Milanese told me that in Sicily
  He heard Africa's drums
I hear them, too,
   especially when
   from across the little stretch of gleaming sea
   North African winds
   blow through our homes

Sicilians left for other lands
trying to escape poverty   injustice
   they prayed to their
   Black Madonna of Tindari

miraculous advocate for the poor
for guidance
packing her image with their clothes

In America at first
they called us colored
Sicilians lynched in the South
    along with Africans
    in the fields, the railroads, the mines,
    the children and grandchildren of slaves
    worked at our sides
    taught us American life
    were thought good people,   even friends

In America over the years
Sicilians stayed quiet   spoke English
    learned to stand apart
    from those darker sisters and brothers
Sicilians passed to that lighter
    opportunity side of the color line

In America now
some of the Black Madonna's children
    have forgotten her
    ignorant of their roots
    they check the box for white on every form
    no longer aware
    that they are of mixed blood
    the mongrel heirs
    to a proud people of every feature

I cannot forget
when even my teeth tell our story

I will not forget
I have prayed at the Black Madonna's
    ancient, wind-swept shrine at Tindari

I am Sicilian
I am not white.

THE STAIRS

My mother remembered that
on the Sunday after the United States entered
the Second World War
my grandfather was painting the house stairs
the radio announced that German U-Boats were spotted off
the New York coast

My grandfather stopped mid-way on the stairs
he asked, "Why am I painting these stairs at a time like this?"
He shook his head, continued to paint
answering his question:
because the stairs needed painting
because we go on
because despite a war
we must eat, work, make love
because there is a need for home and shelter
    amidst the terror

I ask myself, "Why am I reading poems at a time like this?"
because poems need to be read
because we go on
because despite a war
we must eat, work, make love
because there is a need for music and poetry
    amidst the insanity of greed and governments

Because life on earth   in the universe
  is matter
  is energy
that will not be destroyed.

CIVIL RIGHTS

My grandmother and I sat in her Jersey living room
    watching the Civil Rights Movement on TV
I was a little girl, she middle aged
she'd come to the States from Sicily
after the Second World War
she never mastered the jumpy, twisty
tongue of English and this pained her

We sat and watched brave children walking to school
    surrounded by angry mobs
we watched the marchers, the lunchcounter sit-ins,
the voting registrations, the sheriffs, the dogs
the full force of fire hoses turned on people
knocked to the sidewalk

"Perchè?" my grandmother asked. She wanted to
 know why this was happening
"They want to vote, Nonna,
They want to go to whatever schools and restaurants they want"
"Why can't they? They were born here
I can go anyplace I want and I can't speak English
I can vote and I can't speak English
Why can I when they cannot?
This is injustice!"
"Their people were once slaves, Nonna"
"And we were always sharecroppers, almost slaves,
to the Duke D'Averna
These people are the real Americans"

I remember that my grandmother never mentioned color
the TV newspeople kept saying "Negroes"
All she saw were Americans
who worked here
who spoke English

Nonna knew Mussolini had grabbed Abyssinia
she knew the words to the song "Faccetta Nera"
she knew Sicilian men had gone to Ethiopia to work
married the pretty women there
she knew a relative they called L'Africano
who worked and loved in Africa
he bragged how wonderful it was there

Now in the States, her adopted country
Now in what she thought was the land of liberty
my grandmother was astounded, horrified
at the images on TV
she kept saying
"I was not born here
I cannot speak English
yet I can vote, go wherever I want
Why can I when they cannot?
This is injustice."

FIREWORKS ON JULY 4, 2004

My brother stands legs apart in the dark
his shadowy figure
reminds me of our father
now more than ten years dead

My brother sets off holiday fireworks
in the hot, humid air:
glaring starbursts of color
tall jets of flame and smoke
shrill earsplitting sounds

I think of the bombardment of Iraq
the startling destruction of lives and homes
amidst the blasts of fire and noise

My brother lights up little tanks and tiny missile carriers
that careen up the street and explode
with shrieks and flames

There are soldiers, insurgents, freedom fighters
halfway around the planet this July Fourth
righteous or scared   unsure or deliberate
they fight with fire and noise

When our father returned from the Second World War
    wounded in action
    twenty-three years old
    with a purple heart and a back full of shrapnel

—
33

he went to see the holiday fireworks
with our mother, her sister, and her parents

The fire and the noise flashed him back
to the terrible battles he'd fought in France
he ran, ducked, dived for cover
our mother, her parents, her sister ran after him
shouting
"The war is over!"
"You are home!"
"You are safe!"
"These are only fireworks!"

I pray that one day
all soldiers, insurgents, freedom fighters
will stand and watch fireworks
with children and loved ones at their sides
as our father eventually did
they will recognize as he finally did

   they are safe and home

   these are only fireworks

   the war is over.

PHOTO OF MY MOTHER AND ME

I get for my birthday
 a tortoise shell frame
 with a tiny black and white photo
 of my mother and me
 taken decades ago in a seaside photo booth

I remember

 We are on vacation
 colored lights on whirling rides
 the fragrance of salt ocean and roasted peanuts
 music in an evening sky
 men in light suits and aftershave
 women in summer frocks and high heels
 children in fancy dress-up clothes
 we all stroll the Atlantic City Boardwalk

My mother and I pop into the tight little booth
 for a photograph
 a seabreeze wafts through the curtains
 as Mommy puts in the coins
 and pulls me close

We smile at the automatic flashes

My mother is glamorous with ruby earrings
and swept back shiny black hair
she wears an elegant dress

I am a little geek with pussycat eyeglasses
in a dress with tiny roses and peterpan collar

Smiling for the camera
  with a snaggletoothed grin
I am supremely happy
because this beautiful young woman is my mother
she loves me holds me safe in her lap
giving me confidence
to see beauty wherever we find it
giving me strength
to savor the passing moments of living and
to prize this tiny photograph.

DRAWING STARS

My mother taught me to draw stars
one afternoon in the bright kitchen
window panes frosted over
December holiday time:

My mother is starting a marinara sauce
peeling the garlic   chopping the onion
I sit at the kitchen table
with pencil, paper, crayons, scissors, glitter, glue
not quite five
excited, intense, intent on drawing stars
I squeeze the pencil tight
it races around, trails, stops
droopy, crazy lines   no stars

I plead with my mother to show me how
she carefully places the pencil between my fingers
puts her hand
   sweetly fragrant with garlic and onion
over mine
as she guides me up and down
   over and across   up and down again
teaching me to draw stars
together we draw
   five point Christmas stars
   six point Stars of David
we stop and admire them

I open my crayon pouch of pink paisley fabric
   my mother has made for me

I love that it opens and closes
   with a green ribbon drawstring
inside are all my crayons   new and old
all the best colors
for all the beautiful stars I will make

I slowly draw stars on my own
   five point Christmas stars
   six point Stars of David
I color them, paste glitter on, cut them out
later we hang them
on the indoor orange tree from Sicily
where at the top an angel sits

A half century later
the boss loses her patience with me
she must let me go from the job
she cannot teach me to go as fast as she wants
on all the tasks I try to do
intense, intent on doing the job
I wanted to learn how to speed through the job

yet all my best lessons
learned so long ago
have been of slowness
               patience
               striving for beauty
just as when my mother and I sat
at the kitchen table
drawing stars.

GRADE SCHOOL

At home
my parents made sure we took baths every night
  and scrubbed our hair
  and cleaned our nails and teeth
  dusted ourselves with powder to smell sweet

In school
the sisters asked if we ever bathed
  in our dark rowhouses
  did we have lights?
  what did we eat beside spaghetti and garlic?

At home
we kissed the bread if it ever fell to the floor
my father peeled the fruit with his knife
  and gave us each a piece
  and told us about Sicily
my mother told us that Gesuzzu
  and his mother, the Madonna,
  were kind and loving
  the saints were close to us
  like our dead relatives
  always looking out for us
my grandmother said we should be good
  not act like spoiled americans
  we did not want to make the Madonna cry

At school
I was always scared

—

I thought the sisters said
the church was all about punishment
long, uncountable years of burning
  in purgatory
  or worse
  burning forever in hell
there were rules for everything
the sisters said "Obey! Obey!"
none of us was ever going to be good enough for God
we would have to burn in purgatory
for a long time

At school
the sisters made us sing about Ireland
"the land of our fathers"
not mine
my grandfather said St. Patrick was a Roman
the sisters made mistakes
I was too scared to tell them
I was too scared to breathe
afraid to cough in church
even when I had bronchitis
I passed out in a pew holding in a cough

At school
the sisters told us Italians could be janitors
someone asked if Italians could be teachers
No. They could work in the pizza parlor
Italians could make chewing gum in a factory
  Italians were greasy
  they sweated a lot

Who were they talking about?
Not me
Not my family
the sisters kept making mistakes
I was too scared to tell them

At home
we loved Gesuzzu
and his mother, the Madonna
our Guardian Angels were Italian
they sang opera
Italians were artists
  like Leonardo, Michelangelo, and my father
Italians were doctors
  like Cousin Guglielmo, Dr. Coppolini, and
  Uncle Vincenzo's niece, Maria
you could do whatever job you wanted
the saints would help you

At home
my mother pinned a red cloth, a horn
  and a Blessed Mother medal under my uniform
the nuns had evil eyes
our neighbor, Annina, Salvatore's mother,
cursed a nun once
because Sister would not allow her son
to go to the toilet when he asked
he came home wet everyday
Annina went to the school
to tell the teacher to let Salvatore go when he asked
the nun pushed Annina out of the room

Annina got so mad
she forgot the English words
she cursed the nun in Italian:
"May you have nails wherever you have hair"
some children gasped
the nun smirked
she didn't know the power
of a mother's curse

At home
my mother told me heaven listens to a mother's words
    even if the sisters did not

At home
my father told me the nuns would be punished later
he told me
when I was at school
I should remember to be brave
like Garibaldi's redshirts in Sicily.

translation:
"Gesuzzu"= little Jesus

THE CAPTAIN OF THE SAFETIES

Sister Euphrasia, the eighth grade teacher,
said Italians were irresponsible
  but I was an exception

She counted on me
  to run errands
  tabulate grades
  do her roll book
  handle money

Sister Euphrasia said I was
different than most Italians
  who were dishonest
different than my Italian classmates
  who were lazy

I was smart, responsible
I was the Captain of the Safeties

I had a red book
with all the safety patrol members' names
I put a mark against their names
  if they were not at their posts
  if they did not have their badges on straight
  if they forgot an item of the regulation uniforms
  white shirt, blue tie, blue pants for boys
  white blouse, blue jumper, blue beanie for girls

Sister Euphrasia said
the beanie symbolized a girl's modesty

—

the safeties must set an example
most of the marks against the girl safeties
were for beanie violations

I secured my beanie tight with bobby pins
so even the strongest winds did not blow it off the head
of the Captain of the Safeties

One day my beanie disappeared
maybe it was stolen
maybe it was lost
but it was a disaster

at home I cried and cried
my mother gave me money for another
I cried harder
I would have to buy a new beanie
from Sister Euphrasia
who then would know that
even the Captain of the Safeties
was an irresponsible Italian

My grandmother, a seamstress,
told me not to cry
she knew how to make a beanie
my grandfather gave her
his best blue workpants for material
she worked all night
fashioning a hat
that fit me perfectly and
looked exactly like a regulation beanie

except for the inside where
my grandmother placed a thick cloth hatband
not the regulation leather band

The next day and everyday
until the end of the school year
I wore my imposter beanie

The Captain of the Safeties
was determined
that nobody
would ever see the inside of the beanie

Sister Euphrasia
would never know
that I, too, was an irresponsible Italian.

LAURA

I was an awkward kid of eleven
and teenaged Laura's biggest fan

In July
I sat on the white marble steps of Jessup Street
I watched Laura play ball
all arms and legs and dark wild hair
wearing her brother's mitt
She would jump, catch a high fly
spin and throw the ball
halfway down the block
tan arms and black eyes
lean shoulders, round breasts
Laura sometimes winked at me and smiled
I froze, managed a wave, a show of teeth
I was an awkward kid of eleven
and teenaged Laura's biggest fan

In August
Laura's mother died
She threw much slower
She hardly moved when a ball flew over her head
My heart jumped when she gazed at me
Dark circles weighted her eyes
I ached when I saw the tears on her cheeks
I never said anything
I was an awkward kid of eleven
and teenaged Laura's biggest fan

In September
the neighbor ladies said
Laura had to be the lady of the house
they tsked their tongues
when Laura walked the block with ball and glove
"It's a shame she lost her mother
but it's a disgrace
for a girl her age
to play ball
She has a house to keep
She has to cook for her father and brother"

On October Saturdays
I waited on the marble steps of Jessup Street
for a glimpse of Laura
She didn't come out so often now
except to shop, go to highschool, sweep the sidewalk
She'd smile at me
my heart pounded
I'd wave and grin

I never told her
I was sorry she was sixteen and grown
and could never play ball again
I was an awkward kid of eleven
and teenaged Laura's biggest fan.

VALENTINE TEEN DANCE AT THE AQUARAMA

Many Valentines ago
we danced at the Aquarama

Entwined, slowly moving
we kissed by the octopus tank
Sweetheart, I knew we were dying for love

Red paper hearts floated above filtered water
Clouds of cigarette smoke fogged
the glass home of fresh water fish

Cupid posters and tile floors
silver arrows and the walls
swam in red and black light,
spearmint scent and sweat

We danced past the eels
and the one forlorn shark
Sweetheart, I thought we were dying for love

Many Valentines later
you and the Aquarama
the eels, the shark, and the fish
    all are gone

Sweetheart, I thought we were dying for love

            but we were just young
            we were just dying.

APPARITION

As a child I was afraid the Blessed Mother
  Our Lady Dressed in Blue
might appear to me, her namesake,
she would come with a terrible message
  I would have to tell the world
  live in a convent with nuns
  meaner than the ones
  who were my teachers
  I'd scrub endless marble floors
  like poor Bernadette of Lourdes

No more macaroni, no more soda
just holy water to drink and one communion wafer a day

The Blessed Mother dictated letters
  to Lucia of Fatima
the first two were about world wars
the third so horrifying
the Pope fainted when he read the words
  told Lucia she had to stay locked up
  never to repeat the message to anyone

I prayed to the Madonna
begging her not to appear to me
  even though I was named for her
  I wasn't holy enough
  I hoped she did not like me
  because I chewed gum, whistled,
  said curse words, punched my brothers

Now in mid-life
I would welcome an apparition
I pray each day to
the uncompromising Mother
the powerful and just Black Madonna of Tindari

She may appear to me anytime
I am not scared   I am ready
she can tell me disasters
  I will listen
no matter the toughness of her demands
  I'd tell the world the terrible and true
  in admiration of her goddess strength

I have swords in my own heart now

She can come.

GRADUATION (for Rosario Famà)

My father went to my university graduation
          alone

I was in Sicily
in love with his native land
where he could not afford
to go beyond the fifth grade

"Che peccato!" the school examiners said
he was so smart
a shame he could not
continue his education

My father went to my university graduation
          alone
he read the program
found my name on the list
of honors graduates
listened to the speakers

I was traveling
I had studied at the university in Rome
I had studied at the university in America
my father's adopted land
where he got a job because
"school is for babies," his father said
yet he kept on reading
filling his mind with literature, music, art

My father went to my university graduation
        alone
I was the first of his children to graduate
he picked up my degree
kept it on his desk
till I returned months later

I placed it in the bookcase he made
to hold his favorite books

the degree was mine and his.

        .

translation:
"Che peccato!"=What a shame!

GHAZAL #1

Standing on the stage I banish stage fright
tell my reality in the spotlight

My father and three brothers in the park
wave as they catch the wind for my new kite

Melissa said she petted a cornsnake
"He looked like a handbag but felt alright"

We dance in Athens at Easter time
circling Zitagma Square hands held tight

Earrings you gave me hurt at the party
My ear lobes bled although we did not fight

Dreams of Italy: movie star faces,
the pasta plates, wine bottles shining bright

Perfumed with Fendi, I fry the fishes
cook tortellini, cookbook out of sight

A pregnant belly resting on my thighs
knees on pubic hair, baby moves all night

A New York frame holds my papyrus sheet:
Sicilian Syracuse in Greek light

Handstitched poems of Gibran, Roman postcards,
a blue denim shirt fill me with delight

"Good thoughts must come through the left hand shoulder"
A Navajo told me to balance right

Carpentry in nylons, poems in overalls
my name sings of woman's bittersweet insight.

BEHIND THE CAMERA

I am silent behind the camera
just an eye attached to the lens

I film the courtroom scenes
and love the judge
whose full throated voice
sings through my body

I record
her decisions on motions
recalling her motions beneath the black robe

I film
as she listens
her dark hair falling across her forehead

I focus
as her brown eyes scan plaintiff, defendant,
jurors, lawyers, witnesses

I am silent behind the camera
an eye on an eyepiece
turning my camera toward action

the judge nods at me with a smile

I am her eye.

6:35 A.M.

Saturday morning   subway train
lady next to me reads the Koran
Arabic on one page   English on the other
window seat man scans The Watchtower
Jehovah Witness magazine
aisle woman reads her Bible
somebody hums a gospel tune
I say a rosary in my head
my tongue makes the sign of the cross
inside my head
the way my father taught me to do
so no one can tell   when I pray.

MY WATCH

My watch is losing time
    its steps slower than ever
    not like when
    it ran on Tuscan hilltops
    and would not walk
    like Italian clocks do.

Little mechanical heart of time,
for so long
your pulse has been strapped to mine
your wheels spinning
my blood pacing
we beat together
    through Aegean towns and Philadelphia alleys
    in strange beds and familiar clothes.

I worry as you age
I fear more for your death than my own
though I sense the slowing of
my muscles in your measured hands
gears and guts grind, wear away
faded cheeks
wrinkled eyes
glance at your weathered face.

My watch is losing time
    and I wind and set the hands
    ten minutes ahead
I know I cannot stop its decline

nor stem the curve of my own pained hand
when I say with the passing seasons
    that chronology is a lie.

PART THREE

SPIRIT WORLD

. . . .

A MORNING GHAZAL

Arise to gentle fire; morning's first light
start with a prayer and the sky's delight.

I open the kitchen door to blue sky
reverence for the snow that fell last night.

Feeding bread to the sparrows and starlings,
I watch for dark feathers in the snow's white.

Teabags of ginger peach tea from China
an expensive brew to sip winter light.

The dears that have gone to another realm
left paintings, photos, and books for my sight.

I want to give proper gifts to my dead:
quiet, serene respect and love's insight.

Wrestling with the morning's metaphors
I squeeze poetry's raw syllabic might.

By noon I give thanks for winter sunshine's
graceful shadows, start the soup for tonight.

I am named for my grandmother, use my mother's pot,
vegetables and poems for the living and dead, I chop and recite.

BIRTHDAY POEM 2 FOR ANITA

Courageous   Honest
Long spears of words   Short knives of talk
     I love you fiercely
    That's the long and short of it
Long   Short
Don't ever be away too   Take shortcuts home
Long   Short
long time   slice away minutes
longing   not longing
     I love you fiercely
    That's the long and short of it

    Measure
   I can never measure
   the time of soaring
   beyond long hours
   behind the longing

   Kindred Spirit
   I say you are my
   lofty kind generous deep
   Kindred Spirit

   Mind Massage
   Hand Massage
    Messages
   in script, in gift, in tone
   Strong Messages
   I can never measure

                    I love you fiercely
The spin of eternity   The verve of the hour
                    A vigorous flow
Earnest and bold   Quick and fleet
in High   in Ebb
                    Tides form
                    the lithe tie
                    of kindred spirits

Our Best Selves give warmth in all seasons
I love you fiercely in the long and short of it.

AUGUST HEAT

We buried you in August heat
in summer black we sang you home
"How Great Thou Art," "Amazing Grace," and "Peace,"
filing past your lifeless face and stony hand.
"Don't let them lay me out," I knew you'd once said
long ago I'd replied, "Your family owns the body when
    you're dead."

My dear, I could not stand to see you dead
I collapsed, I cried in the morning heat
I shook, I gasped for air; "Have courage" the priest said.
How could it be you were in a better home
than the one where you were near at hand?
I wept and heard them tell you, "Rest in peace."

I have all the letters you signed, "my love and peace,"
ironic now that you are dead
your dying by your own calm hand
you left and never said goodbye in August heat
drinking a deathly sleep in a rowhouse home
cuddling a green pillow, all the reasons never said.

When I first saw you lying there, "I'll let her sleep," I said
"She's tired," I thought, "She could use a little peace."
You'd read the paper, the TV set was on, it seemed like home
then I saw the mug, the pills and smelled the scent of the dead
I felt the chill of fear in the high summer heat
I shook you feeling warmth in your still hand

I stroked your hair searching for the pulse in your still hand
I tried to breathe some life in you and "Why?" and "Why?" I said.
The ambulance came but you had died in August heat,
the policemen and the detectives disturbed the peace
with the questions over and over, no questions answered on
    why you were dead
the police photographer snapped a picture of a death at home.

Your father, your brother, my brother, and I standing at home
sobbing as police pull the rings from your hand
rigor mortis set in and we saw you beautiful even dead.
His work done, "Get me a sheet," the medical examiner said.
I searched for the best, the seashell gift in beige, to wrap you
    in peace,
in the sheet you'd given me they carried you into the heat.

Now much later you come to me in dreams at home,
with a knowing smile, a brilliant eye, and a steady hand,
you tell me it is fine and no big deal to be dead.
In August heat we laid your body down
seeking the peace in each season's promise
and through the years in the said and unsaid prayers
    for understanding

WHY I DON'T PLAY THE GUITAR ANYMORE

My fingers freeze
there is hurt on the strings
heartache on the fret
memory unfolds one stark day

While I was strumming STREETS OF LAREDO
she was making soup in her just a week dead mother's kitchen
ironing her freshly widowed father's shirts

While I was practicing ROLL OVER BEETHOVEN
she was home writing a note, swallowing pills
beginning her sleep toward death

While I was noting chords laughing with my band
she was caressing a green pillow
her brain slowing   her mind slipping away

While I rode the subway home tapping out rhythms
her heart stopped

While I walked in the door with my guitar
seeing her there, thinking her asleep
her spirit might've watched me tiptoe
trying not to make a sound
putting down the guitar
taking tortellini out of the fridge for supper
wondering if I had time
to buy her favorite sugared taralli

When I moved the guitar
             I saw the note   the cup   the pills
my guitar case   so heavy   so black
an explosion   in my head   my heart

the world turned upside down

I could not revive her
the music   inside my head
      a dirge
joking policemen   gawking neighbors   the coroner

her body carried out
my guitar case   my heart   so heavy   so black
the music   a dirge.

JEANS JACKET

                             I know you are dead
Hanging clothes, packing clothes
folding and sorting clothes
                             I know you are dead
I open the drawer   you are dead
I close the drawer   you are dead
in the closet out of the closet you are dead

But where is your jeans jacket?
the jacket I loved redolent of you, the elegant chef
  the faded denim contained your world
  extra-virgin olive oil soaked the blue fibers
  the fabric breathed garlic cloves and Tatiana perfume

I never pictured you dead   wiry, strong, and resilient
                       wearing the jacket till
                       the first deep snow

                       you must've given it away
                       before you died in August heat
                             without a word

If I had the jacket
I'd stroke, pat and fondle each cotton strand
I'd rub it like a genie's lamp
cuddle and place it under my pillow for dreams and poems
                       you are dead
the jacket survives you
on some other one

far away or down the street
                            you are dead
A dreamer wears it on the job
                            you are dead
A teenager strolls the mall in it
                            you are dead
the jacket's on an artist, a housewife, a revolutionary

feeling restless in the night
searching for art and understanding
cooking and sewing and playing the piano
                            I know you are dead
I hang sort fold the clothes
                            I know you are dead
                            and wandering still.

ANITA ON THE TELEPHONE

Love, you call me in my dream
on a telephone line crackling with static
from the land of the dead

>   You say you are around above and below
>   You want me to follow the Tao Te Ching

Love, you remember my Lao Tsu devotion
my way was physics and the Tao until you died
and I forgot and all was struggle

>   You call from the land of shades
>   to remind me
>   "Hold fast to the center, love"

>   I argue that I try
>   but my insides shake

>   You say be like water
>   "The highest good is like water"

>   I recall the flow and the Tao
>   You say
>   "Being great, it flows
>   It flows far away
>   Having gone far, it returns"

Love, I cannot hold you on a crackling line
When I awake I take from the shelf the Tao Te Ching

I cradle this book
I have not read in seven years
I read and hear
your voice through the static
repeating the lines

I say aloud with you
"Though the body dies,
The Tao will never pass away."

SUMMERSTORM 1993

Humidity and heat and salty tears

My father died in late Spring
  Roses cut from his hand-made trellis
  in a vase by his bed

Thunder and lightning and choking voices

My father said he saw his mother's face
  on the ceiling of the hospital
  on the day of his operation
  He said he'd sketched her quickly
  before the anesthesia

Electric sparks and sulfur smell
The air is thick with rain

We pack away my father's clothes
  the pockets yield
  scribbled Sicilian proverbs and musical notations
  snatches of poetry and the Bible
  thumbnail sketches of flowers and faces

An explosion of light and sound

We find my father's last drawings
his view from the hospital room
high rises, William Penn and City Hall
and the tiny sketch of a woman

My grandmother's slanted black eyes
her firm mouthed gaze
her white hair wind-blown
younger looking than when she died

My father saw his mother's face
  on the ceiling of the hospital

She was brave, not angry
She was waiting

Clean breezes and fresh clarity
the air is dry
the sky is indigo
with stars.

THE SCENT OF AFTERSHAVE

A scent of aftershave sometimes fills rooms
sweet bracing clean comforting

it is my father's spirit visiting

My aunt smells aftershave in her kitchen
while peering into a pot of sauce
she turns to see if someone climbed the backstairs
No, she knows it is her brother visiting

My mother awakens to aftershave in her winter bedroom
she questions the sheets, "Is it detergent?"
No, she knows it is her husband visiting

My father was a barber
every morning he splashed aftershave on himself
then onto customers in his shop
he took aftershave from his traveling barber case
when he gave haircuts and shaves
in offices, bedrooms, parlors, kitchens, and cellars

The scent of aftershave fills my parlor
as I drink tea and face a stack of bills
I rush out the front door   no one is passing
no scent of aftershave outside

in the parlor my father's fragrance lingers
he is visiting
"Daddy, Daddy," I whisper, "You are here."

PART FOUR

UNDER THE TENT
PERFORMANCE POEMS

. . . .

LOOKING FOR COVER

We are carbon based life forms
       with skin, hats, and scarves
       aprons, sweaters, and coats
       gloves, socks, and boots

We are cosmic
       with tablecloths and pillowcases
       slipcovers and doilies

We spin
       under canvas, leather, and wood
       brick, glass, and steel

Fragile and great
       with stardust and greenery
       the air of the ages surrounds us
       as we look for cover and
       put down our words

       in whatever script
       on paper and stone with ink and laser

       Carbon and Cosmic
       We look for cover.

ERAVAMO A NAPOLI

Nobody remembers the poet but me

Eravamo a Napoli
Johnny, Julie, Joy, Mike and me

We ate pizza napoletana
    nella pizzeria
    high up a flight of stone steps

The poet sold his poems from a shopping cart
He pushed it from table to table:

Want a love poem? Cento lire
Amore, Amore, vita mia

Want a war poem? Cento lire
Guerra, Guerra, la battaglia

You like flowers? Fiori rossi per te
Are you religious? O Santa Madonna
Cento lire, cento lire

We laughed
I knew he was a real poet

Eravamo a Napoli
Johnny, Julie, Joy, Mike, and me
eating pizza con funghi, pizza con mozzarella
drinking wines golden and ruby
high on hashish

We laughed
I knew he was a real poet

He pushed the shopping cart closer
How about a nice love poem for her?
He pointed to me

Who? We laughed. Who?

I asked the brown eyes in his neat bald head
Want a drink? I'm a poet, too.
What kind? All kinds.

Eravamo a Napoli
Johnny, Julie, Joy, Mike, and me
We laughed
Our mouths full of pizza
    reeking of hash
    dizzy with wine

The soccer match was on TV
Cheers! Cheers! Napoli! Napoli!

Nobody remembers but me
how he made up a poem
standing there with his cart
guzzling white wine: Eravamo a Napoli quando

There were twenty communist students at other tables
    in red socks and red shirts
They sang the Internationale

Eravamo a Napoli
Johnny, Julie, Joy, Mike, and me
The poet sold his poems only to me
   per mille lire
I bought the complete set of love poems

Amore, amore, vita mia

He recited a few for me
Belle I said Meravigliose
Grazie he said

He was a real poet and
Nobody remembers but me

Eravamo a Napoli
I lost the poems
the complete packet of love poems
in the hotel, on the bus, by the bay
   I don't know
Amore, amore, vita mia
I don't remember the poet's name

Eravamo a Napoli
Johnny, Julie, Joy, Mike, and me.

WATCHING DIZZY GILLESPIE ON TV

Dizzy Dizzy
Chipmunk sweet Chipmunk blow sweet notes
Notes blue and hot and cool and bop do what

Do scat with Hendricks just hands
hands and mouth
hand to microphone to mouth to phone
phone do phone do phone do saxophone

Due due due due what
what dues are due due due we we we
try to be so cool together
paying dues be dues

Bop Do Bop Do Bop Do Bop Do We

We when we when we when
We saw each other last
it felt right right oh right alright
nothing holding back do back do back due
We you we you we you
You called me back, do back, due show
do show it was a shadow a shadow
in your voice I thought trouble trouble
Trouble and oooh and oooh ooh ooh

sweetheart sweetheart
I can't can't can't
get through through through

81

I told you you you you you
love love love I love love love
you be do you be do
but you but you oooh you
said yes, oh yes, yes, yes
and what I thought and what
the hell does that mean?
you said it sweet yes yes and yes and yes
But Bay Be Bay Be Babe Be Bay you
Wha wha wha what can it mean?

Za Za Za Za
Max Roach is on the High Hat Cymbal
High Hat Hi Hi High High Hat
Za Za Za MMMMNNNN Zim Zim
Zimma Zimma Zimma Zimma
Simmer Simmer Simmmerrr
I'm scared and mad and mad
and scared and wha wha wha why
Zim Zim do zim do zim do do
do do do you just say yes
and not I love you, too, too, too, toooeeee
Zimm who's there Zimm who's there Zim with you
Do zista so zista do zista
Dissa Dissa Zimma Diss Diss Diss
Disappeared you went and disappeared
off the line
Behind the dip do dip do dip zim zim
and I can't say love oh love oh love
and now I say yeah baby yeah baby
yeah baby do dit do dik do dik you

zim bad zim bad another sister hey sister
like in grade school all I could say was
yes sister yes sister yes sister
scared and mad yes sister

Gerry Mulligan is playing hothot hot hot
The Hot Society Hot Society
old clips of Charlie Parker
The Bird flying flying flying
flying and he's dead on the videotape
To To To Toooh Bad la la la la
Zim do zim sweet sweet sweet

I try to write right write right
write right oh do do do you you
are you scared
some people will say you
go with a nut
Tut Tut Tut Sax Saxo Saxo
Saxophone oh that phone phone
phone the last phone call and then
you diss diss diss disappeared

Frank Foster and Dizzy on the special
Dizzy on the special   on the horn
horn horn that special special horn
oooh oooh oooh a phone
The Night in Tunisia
wind blow hot wind blow hot
wind in the phone sax oh sex oh phone
wind wind wind and win win win

win a song from the des from the des
from the desert the desert the des des
desk win a pub pub pub do zim
do zim publishing contract tracts
on track on zim do zim do
tract tract tract tract

Ter ter ter ter teres teres teresa
Teresa was a sa sa sa saint
Saint Teresa   Saint Teresa Saint Teresa of Avila
wrote she wrote she wrote a lot
lot lot lot lot do zim do tracts do wha
about she wrote about
an angel piercing her heart heart heart
with a with a with a
flaming flaming flaming arrow
whoa whoa whoa whoa
They made her a saint

Dizzy play Dizzy play St. Dizzy
play Charlie Bird Charlie Bird
Charlie Bird Parker is a saint
is a saint do phone do phone do saxophone
whoa whoa oh woe woe woe
Dizzy'll be Dizy'll be
be bop do bop be bop be be
A Saint
Trumpet cool Trumpet hot
do what do what flaming arrow trumpet
hot do hot be bop be bop cool
cool coolie oh coolie oh

could could could
They make me a saint?

Do saint do dosaint 'cause I write
about your yes oh yes oh yes and the pain
and the hot do hot of hurt and
chest heart oh chest heart hurt
do hot hurt do hot
Zimm and the Zimm and the Zim
when the phone hangs up and the
line is cold and you're gone
and gone and gone and cool cool
cool and cold and cold and
the words words words are all
brok brok brok en en en
oh do you do you broken and the heart
and the heart is pow is pow pow pow
do what do what
is power and be oh be oh
love love love lovely lovely
and zim crash zim crash and zim

The comets come round they
come round and around and around
and around and get famous
do I do I do I do I do I
wa wa wa want to
be famous yes famous and
no no no no no no no
noticed and walk and write
and walk and do bop do bop

do bop and be read oh read
oh ready yes ready and read

Dizzy, oh St. Dizzy oh
St. Dizzy we working all
the same and saying and playing
and swinging and singing
Do Dizzy St. Dizzy oh
and it's all be do be do be
do be bop oh bop do zim
about love and love and yes.

WALKING ON ICE

ice   oh   ice

Wind-shaped   crystal-cracked

White smiling visitation
Clear and Dangerous

ice   oh   ice
           I am afraid

There are doings and undoings in the universe
I step into cold, dark space

Planets veer off course
Stars go nova

ice   oh   ice
           I am afraid

Rickety ankles in legwarmers
driven by fragile bone skull

I step onto frozen star gas and dust

Slick blackholes await

ice   oh   there is ice

           on the earth

in the heavens

I slide on the Milky Way

I am afraid.

THE FALLS

There are many Falls on this earth
Niagara Falls and Angel Falls
majestic cascading flowing
Falls, Falls, I have known Falls
I have fallen in the best of places
Falls, Falls
I fell on the icy iron steps of my grammar school
sitting for hours with bleeding knees
Falls, Falls
I fell in front of the Archdiocesan Office
the day I signed up to work Philly's Catholic Schools
Falls, Falls
I fell in front of Temple University's Law School
tearing my left leg's ligaments

Falls, Falls
There are many Falls on this earth
Minnehaha Falls and Iguassu Falls
majestic cascading imposing
Falls, Falls, I have known Falls
I have fallen in the best of places
Falls, Falls
I fell off a chair at an outdoor café
cracking my head on sidewalk cement
Falls, Falls
I fell down my home's cellar stairs
banging my rump down half a dozen steps
Falls, Falls
I fell in the parking lot after seeing The Aviator film
ripping my jeans   bruising my back

Falls, Falls
There are many Falls on this earth
Victoria Falls and Marmore Falls
majestic cascading powerful
Falls, Falls, I have known Falls
I have fallen in the best of places
Falls, Falls
I fell over the threshold of my fourth grade classroom
on my first day of teaching
tearing my stockings   black and blue laughter
Falls, Falls

Falls, Falls
I fell down the marble steps of the Vatican Museum
my skirt flying around my chest
my arms circling my head
a human barrel rolling down down down
landing at the bottom   my Roman Miracle of No Broken Bones
Falls, Falls
I fell at a fancy restaurant as I was introduced
to give a poetry reading to the Sicilian American Club
slipping then sliding sideways across the dance floor
stopping at the foot of the podium
I rose and recited

Falls, Falls
There are many Falls on this earth
Hillawe Falls and Seneca Falls
majestic cascading pounding
Falls, Falls, I have known Falls
I have fallen in the best of places

—
90

Falls, Falls
I fell backwards while boarding a bus
into the strong arms of University of Pennsylvania students
who hoisted me   shaken, jolted, grateful
back into the bus
Falls, Falls
I have known Falls
I have fallen in bars and churches, at weddings and funerals,
    on carpet and wood
I have fallen under cars, out of cars, on ice, leaves, and stone
I have fallen dancing the tarantella, the polka, the waltz
Falls, Falls
I have fallen in the best of places

Falls, Falls
There are many Falls on this earth
Bowen Falls and Woolamumbi Falls
Tower Falls and Ribbon Falls
Shoshone Falls and Imatra Falls
majestic, cascading, pounding, powerful, flowing
Falls, Falls, I have known Falls
I have fallen in the best of places
Falls, Falls
I have known Falls.

OUR EXERCISE

All the Seasons Joey jogs I walk
All the Seasons Joey jogs I walk

Joey jogs
Joey jogs
I walk green red flame trees turning brown
Street stands load pumpkin turkey apple bean candy bars
Joey jogs
Joey jogs
He goes by blue slicker and mustache
I walk and wave in fading tan and fallen leaves

Joey jogs
Joey jogs
I walk stark tall tree limbs of ice
Frozen boxes cram snowcapped yam onion lettuce fennel root
Joey jogs
Joey jogs
He goes by hooded sweatshirt and mustache
I walk and nod in bundled scarf and slushy boot

Joey jogs
Joey jogs
I walk flowery trees white pink orange blossom sky
Chocolate bunnies eggs chicks crowd ripe strawberry lamb
Joey jogs
Joey jogs
He goes by tank-top and mustache
I walk and smile in open coat and mood

Joey jogs
Joey jogs
I walk lush tree balmy breeze and heat
Stands pile plum watermelon peach orange honeydew
Joey jogs
Joey jogs
He goes by sportshorts and mustache
I walk in white cotton tossing off a grin

Joey jogs
I walk
Joey jogs
I walk

All the Seasons Joey jogs I walk
All the Seasons Joey jogs I walk.

THE ROSES

Roses, Roses, Roses
I praise the roses, my flowery friends
roses, roses, roses

I praise all the colors of the roses
roses, roses, roses
sturdy soft and thorny
these roses, roses, roses

I praise Rosette and Rosina
Rosemary and Rosemarie, Rosie, Rosa, and Roe
Roseann, Roselle, Rosalyn, Rosalind, and Rose
Rosaria, Rosalia, and Rosalie
these roses, roses, roses
these poets and lovers
these mothers, godmothers, stepmothers, grandmothers
fragrant, fragrant, fragrant roses, roses, roses
these teachers, singers, cooks, bakers
luscious, luscious, luscious   roses, roses, roses
these musicians, painters, storytellers
roses, roses, roses
these daughters, aunts, nieces, and spouses
dew-kissed sun-kissed perfumed
roses, roses, roses

Roses on the walls   roses in the yards
roses in the offices, classrooms, and malls
these roses, roses, roses
roses in and on and with the hearts

roses in and on and by the beds
roses in and on and by the roads
these roses, roses, roses

I praise and I bless my flowery friends
these roses, roses, roses
I call the Great Ladies of the Roses to bless
the roses, roses, roses
Sweet Saint Rose of Lima with your roses
bless the roses, roses, roses
Doctor Little Flower Saint Therese De Lisieux with your roses
bless the roses, roses, roses
Powerful Saint Rita of Cascia with your roses
bless the roses, roses, roses
Our Amerindian Lady of Guadalupe with your roses
bless the roses, roses, roses

Bless all the roses, roses, roses
Bless these demure, daring, and dazzling
roses, roses, roses.

TO LORCA

Darling
The moon is green tonight
    green, green
    as the streets
    money and trees
    green as all the cars
I cannot   Take off the shades

No, never, baby, never
    green the stars
        and
    green the grass
    green hair
    green lips
    and now I have you green
Never going to   Take off the shades

They're foldable, honey
and they come with a case
    I'm green and cool
    on the green stair
    under green sun
    the sky is green
I will not   Take off the shades

My eyes behind
    the mirror lens

carry green tears
you always see
your glassy face
in green
I dare not   Take off the shades

Apple green
Bread green
Green you
Green me
Fires are green
I can never   Take off the shades.

CONVERSATION

> I want so badly to kiss your hair

It's so lonely inside my head

> I want so badly to kiss your hair

We speak across at cross currents

> I want so badly to kiss your hair

I'm so behind myself in every way

> I want so badly to kiss your hair

Salmon you say
I have a little roasted chestnut head
Subway you say
You have a little golden honey head
The president you say
Wheels spin inside our perfect brains

> Your tan fingers
> through those tangled strands
> to make a point

Money you say
> I want so badly
The seasons you say
> It's so lonely inside

—
98

I want so badly to kiss your hair

Juniper you say
Spruce you say
Walnut you say

I want so badly to kiss your hair.

BACK FROM BALTIMORE

Back from Baltimore
Broad and Snyder, Philadelphia's where
I mail the postcard of the Constellation ship
There's no more in Baltimore
than anywhere else of me
My color is tired
beige and dragging
twilight and numb
burnt past siesta
under Ronald McDonald's red golden flag
Broad Street in tube socks, loafers, and blue denim

Ronald McDonald like the Sacred Heart
arms upraised
blesses all who enter
today's icon
for kids and kin
the kidless and kinless
all inside eating those fries

What else do you do, kid?
Write and write
like when
tired real tired
wrote the spelling words 3 times each
and the times tables
over and over and over
the two to the twelve
the two to the twelve

It's after twelve
I'm tired
all the colors are tired
beige and tan
damp alleyways
glassy bit streets
newspapers and summer
all pass away
clouds and politics
wars and soupcans
food and stars
pass away, pass away
too tired to manage a shrug

The body goes on hold
coming home
staring at the buses
going home from Baltimore
where I couldn't find a stamp
I mail you a card from Broad and Snyder
Philadelphia
going home
tired with windows and doors
mostly closed
curtains in the parlor
cups in the sink
dragging and dragging
maybe the backdoor is still open
for moonbeam sunlight
coaldust crayon leaves telephone lines

If you'd come to Baltimore
I'd've been your guide

But we always want more
not just crumbs

crumbs, crumbs
crumbling away

the house and the walls
are flakes of plaster and brick
alone.

IN LOVE WITH THE LAUNDRY

She had

        Wind and Sun in a city yard
        Clouds in strips against the blue
        A face and hands

        To hang the empty dears
            who
        belonged in warm light
        sighing like fresh bread rising
        smelling of damp morning mountains
                and seashells

She was blown among the sheets
        in love with the laundry

She sucked on clothespins
        savoring their hardness
        their forest fragrance

        They know the ropes

She could only guess at the intimacies of
        the clean white jockey shorts
        innocent and forgetful on the line

She hugged the breezy unstuffed shirts
        their dangling arms around her neck

        and those pants
        how they danced.

—

THE CATERERS IN LOVE

With little garlic kisses and a parsley caress
 oregano scented, we embrace
                              our onion lips parted
                              our basil tongues crushed
                              amid our rosemary sighs

your pepper touch mushrooms my salt breath
my thyme   your sage
                              eggplant eyes
                              a hand of walnuts
                              a hand of chestnuts

cucumber and cabbage heads

we simmer   we nibble

our bay leaf celery corn   our ears, lobes, and knees

arugula neck   zucchini nose   cilantro breasts

bean arm   banana leg

Bellies strawberries nipples   cherries and buns

carrot love   chive love

paprika cinnamon ginger love

in salsa and curries float our artichoke hearts

You are my potato tomato
I am your escarole roll

We fry   bake   and   braise

We steam   We saute

We are bread   We are soup

We are candied yams   We are honey wheat

We are figs

always juicy and sweet.

THE PEOPLE IN HELL

The people in hell want ice water.

> They have brimstone barbecue
>   glorious perfume
>   blue sauna and
>   cable TV

The people in hell want ice water.

> They have hot biscuits
>   saltines
>   clarified butter
>   caviar

The people in hell want ice water.

> They fly first class
> Sleep in hotels with
> vibrating beds
> They've got a planetarium
> They're allowed to vote

The people in hell want ice water.

> They all go by the title of "doctor"
> Wear blazers, wing-tips, and pumps
> They have pennies and cake
>   therapy and hand-guns
>   sportscars, a clam bar

                                                           and
                                             free checking.

Still,
The people in hell want ice water.

SAPPHO

O Sappho   Sap pho   Sappho   Sap pho

you say and I say and you say

"Although they are only breath
words which I command are immortal"

O Sappho   Sap pho   Sappho   Sap pho

I saw my great grandmother dancing dancing dancing
at a Greek Festival
Her face on a young beauty in full costume
the dress the same as the one she wore
in the only photo she ever took
when she was a dimpled girl
in an embroidered headdress

     her face was for kissing
     her feet for dancing

Sappho   Sap pho   Sappho   Sap pho
Greece Sicily   Greece Sicily   Greece Sicily
     lands of light
     una faccia una razza

Nonna Nonna   dancing dancing

Sappho   Sap pho   Sappho   Sap pho

you say and I say and you say

"tender feet of Cretan girls
danced once around an altar of love
crushing a circle in the soft, smooth flowering grass"

O Sappho   Sap pho   Sappho   Sap pho

Nonna Nonna is dancing and turning
turning and dancing toward the light

O Sappho   Sap pho   Sappho   Sap pho

you say and I say and you say

"the full moon is shining
Girls take their places
as though around an altar"

Sappho   Sap pho   Sappho   Sap pho

the moon, O Sappho, the moon
the dance   the kisses   the sea
loves spin   poems dance
by a sapphire sapphic sea

     Greek and Sicilian
     Tyrrhenian, Ionian, Aegean Seas
     the deepest blue
     black eyes and green seas
     sapphire sapphic seas

Sappho   Sap pho   Sappho   Sap pho
the sun of Sicily is the same sun of Lesbos

—
109

Sappho   Sap pho   Sappho   Sap pho
you sang in exile on Etna's isle

Sappho   Sap pho   Sappho   Sap pho
was the Sicilian bread salty in exile?

    Yet the tongue was yours
    the dance was yours
    the yearning for lost loves still yours

O Sappho   Sap pho   Sappho   Sap pho

you say and I say and you say

"Go and be happy
but remember whom
you leave shackled by love"

    gray eyes and brown and sea green
    soft footsteps   flowers in hair

Sappho   Sap pho   Sappho   Sap pho
you the tenth muse
I say to my friend visiting Lesbos
to whisper my name to you
for I have felt Sicilian sun and Greek sun
and viewed the burning stars of night time yearning

O Sappho   Sap pho   Sappho   Sap pho

you say and I say and you say

"Day in, day out
I hunger and I struggle"

O Sappho   Sap pho   Sappho   Sap pho

my great grandmother in the photo in costume
of Sicily   of Greece   of Mediterranean

    her feet turn and skip
    her face smiles and sings

O Sappho   Sap pho   Sappho   Sap pho
in Philadelphia my blood is your blood
if brotherly love is more
if sisterly love is more

Sappho   Sap pho   Sappho   Sap pho

you say and I say and you say

"No voices chanted
choruses without ours
no woodlot bloomed in Spring
without our song"

Sappho   Sap pho   Sappho   Sap pho

    bless me with poems
    show me sun and sea and words
    help me in exile in familiar places
    teach me the songs ancient and new

Sappho   Sap pho   Sappho   Sap pho

you say and I say and you say

"Neither honey nor
the honey bee is
to be mine again"

Sappho   Sap pho   Sappho   Sap pho

you say and I say and you say

"The night is now half gone
youth goes
I am in bed alone"

O Sappho   Sap pho   Sappho   Sap pho
love comes and goes and transcends
    all earthly time

there are women who have gone

Sappho   Sap pho   Sappho   Sap pho

there are women who left our lives

Sappho   Sap pho   Sappho   Sap pho

still we savor the sweet taste
    feel the light touch
    smell the fragrant flesh
    drink the womb's salted sea

O Sappho   Sap pho   Sappho   Sap pho

you say and I say and you say

"You may forget but
let me tell you this:
someone in some future time
will think of us"

O Sappho   Sap pho   Sappho   Sap pho

I saw my great grandmother's face
        on a young Greek American girl
        una faccia una razza
I was a Sicilian American
        at the Greek Festival
        in this new old world

O Sappho   Sap pho   Sappho   Sap pho

        she burns my heart

Sappho   Sap pho   Sappho   Sap pho.

MOTHER HORN: For Rufus Harley

Ma Me Ma Me Ma Me
Rufus Harley didn't think

Ma Me Ma Me Ma Me
It was beneath him
Ma Me Ma Me Ma Me
to play the bagpipes
Ma Me Ma Me Ma Me
to an indifferent lunchtime crowd
Ma Me Ma Me Ma Me
in green and yellow tartan kilt
Ma Me Ma Me Ma Me
All his heart was in the tune

Mom Me Mom Me Mom Me
embracing his difficult mother horn
Mom Me Mom Me Mom Me
Rufus said, "O, Mommy, O"
Mom Me Mom Me Mom Me
is the sound of the bagpipes
O Mommy O Mommy O

Rufus plays so right
Ma Me Ma Me Ma Me
When Mother Horn sings
"Mommy Mommy Mommy
I'm your mother horn mommy

your only own very own
Mommy Mommy Mommy"

Rufus holds on tight
Ma Me Ma Me Ma Me

MY MOTHER'S PRAYER LIST

They asked her
Pray for me
Pray for us
Pray for me
    and she did

My mother kept a list
a long list   a long handwritten list
she kept a long handwritten list
of all those who asked her to pray

She kept a long list
a long handwritten list
until the day she died
when I found the list
the long handwritten list
in her housedress pocket

My mother wrote the names
clear on the page   she wrote the names
in her neat Palmer Method script
she wrote each name followed by a dash
she wrote name, dash, request
of all those who asked her to pray

They asked her
Pray for me
Pray for us
Pray for me
    and she did

She prayed for health, for family, for friends
    for peace in the home
    and peace in the world

She prayed for good marriages, for troubled children
    for surgery survival, for house sales, and school exams

She prayed for courage, for serenity, for patience
    for driving tests, blood tests
    and for finding a job

They asked her
Pray for me
Pray for us
Pray for me
    and she did

My mother cooked, cleaned, went to church, washed clothes,
shopped,
said the rosary, tended the garden
always with the list
the long list the long handwritten list
in her pocket
to help her remember

They asked her
Pray for me
Pray for us
Pray for me
    and she did

in her home   in her gentle way
my mother loved her husband, honored her parents
raised four children
minded grandchildren
always with the list   the long list
the long handwritten list in her pocket

They asked her
Pray for me
Pray for us
Pray for me
    and she did

My mother cooked meals for shut-ins
nursed the sick
mourned the dead
gave comfort   offered courage
always with the list   the long list
the long handwritten list in her pocket

My mother laughed, ate, celebrated
made fabulous cakes and sumptuous dinners
She fed the birds, cared for the cat
swept the sidewalk, watched the stories on TV
she sang, wrote letters, chatted, listened to music
always with the list   the long list
the long handwritten list   in her pocket

Her life was a prayer

They asked her
Pray for me
Pray for us
Pray for me
    and she did

She honored all the requests for prayers
until the day she died
when I found the list   the long list
my mother's long handwritten list
in her housedress pocket
her long handwritten list of all those
who asked my graceful mother to pray

Her life was a prayer

They asked her
Pray for me
Pray for us
Pray for me
    and she did.

COMARI

My comari, my co-marys, my co-marias
Comari, Comari, Comari, Comari
we are rich   we are strong
  in comari tradition
comari, comari, comari, comari
My comari, my co-marys, my co-marias
  I tell you now
  a story of my Aunt
the story of Zia Angelina
proud and regal   with burning black eyes
she had a comare
a dear comare
a beautiful comare   a loving comare
Comare Comare Comare Comare Maria
they lived   they lived two
they lived two doors away
  from each other
these comari comari comari comari
  Angelina e Maria
  Maria e Angelina
They passed   they passed
  they passed
they have since passed
but when   but when
  but when
they were alive
alive alive alive alive
when they were alive
they passed flowered china dishes

filled with delicacies
  to each other
they passed dishes of
  tortellini in brodo
  merluzzo in bianco
  insalata d'arugula
these comari comari comari comari
Comare Angelina   Comare Maria
late afternoons they sipped
  they sipped and dipped
  they sipped espresso
  they dipped biscotti
in late afternoon they sipped and dipped
before before before
  the husbands
before before before
  the suppers
they sipped and dipped
before the suppers and husbands
filled their homes
these comari comari comari comari
They remembered these comari
  each name day
  each birthday
always a greeting card these comari
comari comari comari comari
inside and outside
dishes   coffee   greeting cards
through South Philadelphia streets
far from their Sicilian town
  they made do

they had to
they made do
with dishes   coffee   greeting cards

Once   once   once
Comare Comare Comare Maria's birthday
her birthday was coming
Comare Comare Comare Angelina
made spumetti
she made spumetti from eggwhites and nuts
eggwhites and nuts and sugar
sweets for her Comare Comare Comare Maria
then Angelina went
Comare Angelina went she went
Comare Angelina went to the Avenue to buy a card
a beautiful card   a beautiful birthday card
for her Comare Comare Comare Maria
Angelina read cards that said Happy Birthday
No good   no good   no good
   too plain   too plain
for the beautiful beautiful Comare Comare Comare Maria
Angelina read cards that said Happy Birthday Friend
No good   no good   no good
   no words to describe
the dear, the dearer, the dearest
Comare Comare Comare Maria
Angelina read cards that said Happy Birthday Sister
No good   no good   no good   no good
   too boring, too boring
   not love enough
for the lovely and loving and loved

Comare Comare Comare Maria
Angelina read cards that said Happy Birthday Husband
and there and there and there
   was the perfect card
there was the perfect card
for the beautiful, the dear, the loving
Comare Comare Comare Maria

Angelina bought that card
she bought the To My Dear Husband card
she bought it   and loved it
and took it home
where she took a pen   a black pen
she took a black pen
she crossed out HUSBAND
she crossed that word right out
she crossed out Husband   and wrote COMARE
   in her Italian script
TO MY DEAR COMARE
the words all fit
the words inside and outside
the card   her heart
inside and outside
the words all fit
they fit   she knew they fit
inside and outside
she knew they fit her
Comare Comare Comare Maria
Angelina's Comare Maria.

SANT'ANTONIO: For All Anthonys and Everybody Else

Sant'Antonio   Sant'Antonio   Sant'Antonio Mio
Great Saint Anthony   Great Saint Anthony
I've been praying   praying   praying
to you   you   you   for years
to find me   find me   find me
keys, documents, lovers, books
Saint Anthony, Saint Anthony,
Come around
Something's lost and can't be found
all the lost   all the lost   all the lost you've found
Sant'Antonio Mio
if it's right if it's to be
you've found the lost, lost, lost
and always got me what I needed
Sant'Antonio Mio
St. Anthony   St. Anthony   St. Anthony
come around
St. Anthony called from this way and that way
you covering the earthly continents
and all the galaxies and beyond
finding   finding   finding   the lost, lost, lost
finding even what was not lost
but not yet found
St. Anthony, St. Anthony
come around
will you   will you   will you
find me a job, job, job?
Dear St. Anthony, Anthony, Anthony
Sant'Antonio Mio

jobs, jobs, jobs   I've had and lost many
jobs, jobs, jobs   I've found and lost a lot
jobs, jobs, jobs   I need a new job   a good job
a job, job, job
Sant'Antonio Mio

Great Kind Dear St. Anthony Anthony Anthony
in all the holy pictures   on all the holy medals
in all the holy churches
you are so popular with the populace
Antonio, Antonio, Antonio
Antonio, Anthony, Antony
your name was ancient
even when you roamed the earth
in a physical body
Antonio, Antonio, Portuguese Preacher
shipwrecked in Sicily   settled in Padua
Antonio Antonio Antonio
with your tonsure and Franciscan robe
Saint Anthony of Padua
Antonio Antonio Sant'Antonio Mio
with your golden tongue and bread for the poor
holding the Baby Jesus
just as Hermes held Baby Apollo
Antonius Antonius Antonius
Antony, Anthony, Antonio
Tonio, Ant, Tony, Nino
Ninu, Nini, Nino, Ninuzzu, Nino, Ninitu, Nino
Tony, Tone, Tony
'Ntoni, 'Ntoni, 'Ntoni
Yo, Ant!   Yo, Ant!   Yo, Ant!

Can you find me a miracle job?
Our own only own Anthony   Our St. Anthony
My St. Anthony

Antony, Antoninus, Antinuous, Antonio
all the ancients converge on your name
all those who carry your finding found name
are now and ever converging
Tonio, Ant, Tony, Nino, Tonino
Tony the Tiger, Tony Martin, Tony Taylor, Tony Bennett
Tony fathers, Tony brothers, Tony godfathers, Tony sons
and everybody's Uncle Tony
Yo, Ant!   Yo, Ant!   Yo, Ant!
An Toe Knee Oh   Toe Knee   An Toe Knee Oh
Toe Knee   Toe Knee   Tony, Tony   Toe Knee
St. Anthony   St. Anthony   St. Anthony
your namesakes
are driving buses, publishing books, cutting pecorino
writing mysteries, making gnocchi, film scores, and paintings
Tony with the stethoscope
Tony in the laboratory
Nino, Tony, Anthony, Tonino, Tonio, Tone
pointing to the blackboard
sculpting the clay
genuflecting at the altar
Tony at the keyboard
Tony in the courtroom
Tony with the pen   Tony with the drill
Museum Anthony   TV, Radio, Film Anthony
Anthony Head   Anthony Feet   Anthony Hand
Skinny Tony, Fat Tony, Little Anthony, Big Anthony

Anthony with the Imperials, with the guitars, with the drums
Anthony with Pets, Pizza, and Pomegranates
Anthony with children and the old
Anthony with wives, boyfriends, girlfriends, lovers
Anthony with the stars, sun, and moon
Anthony Rainbow   Anthony Breeze
partner, brother, nephew, cousin, in-law

barber, baker, scientist, crooner, whistler, gardener
Tony with the vow of silence
Tony with the bullhorn
An Toe Knee Oh   An Toe Knee Oh
Tony, Nino, Tone: musician, poet, conductor, journalist,
composer, novelist, gangster, barista   Tony, Nino, Tone

An Toe Knee Oh   An Toe Knee Oh
St. Anthony, St. Anthony,
come around
you, Sweet Antonuccio, you
An Toe Knee Oh
you doll   you honey   you sweetheart
An Toe Knee Oh
An Toe Knee Oh
Please find me that job and all the lost, lost, lost
all the lost music, toys, people
all the lost jobs, money, time
Tony Oh   Tony Oh   Tony Oh
An Thon Eee
An Thon Eee
Saint An Thon Eee
Oh, Anth   Yo, Anth   Oh, Anth

please, please, please
find me   find me   find me
find me that job, job, job
Oh, a job, Oh, a job, Oh, Toe Knee
You can do it
An Toe Knee Oh
An Toe Knee Oh
You can find me a job, a job, Oh, Toe Knee
Sweet Tone   Sweet Tone   Sweet Tone Knee Oh
a job, please   a job, please   a job, please
Toe Knee Oh   Toe Knee Oh   Toe Knee Oh
Sant'Antonio
Sant'Antonio
Sant'Antonio Mio.

ABOUT THE AUTHOR

MARIA FAMÀ is a poet of Sicilian descent. Through publications, books, and readings, she has tried to shape a poetic voice from her experiences as a woman, as an Italian American, and as a participant in a multicultural society. Famà believes that the predominant force in her artistic development was her upbringing in a Sicilian immigrant household. At home, she learned of the Sicilian culture where women were powerful within the home and where she heard from earliest childhood the ritual prayers, traditional teachings, and story-telling poems that were orally transmitted through the generations in this ancient culture.

Famà did her undergraduate and graduate work in History at Temple University, where she also studied Italian and its literature. She studied for one year in Rome, Italy where she more fully discovered her Mediterranean roots. She met relatives in Sicily, lived with a Neapolitan family in Tuscany, and made the strong ties of family and friendship that bind her still to Sicily and Italy.

Maria Famà's books of poetry include *Currents* (Adams Press, Chicago, 1988); *Identification*, first edition, (malafemmina press, San Francisco, 1991); *Italian Notebook* (Hale Mary Press, Syracuse, 1995) written in collaboration with Mary Russo Demetrick; and *Identification*, second edition, (Allora Press, Philadelphia, 1996). Famà's latest poetry manuscript, "Other Nations, An Animal Journal," is being considered for publication. A partial listing of the many anthologies in which her work appears is: *Sweet Lemons* (Legas Press, 2004); *Breaking Open* (Purdue University Press, 2003); *Milk of Almonds* (Feminist Press, 2002); *Identity Lessons* (Penguin Books, 1999); *Curaggia* (Women's Press, 1998); *La Bella Figura: A Choice* (malafemmina press, 1993); and the forthcoming anthologies: *She Is Everywhere, Volume II* and *Women Singing*.

Famà's poetry appears in numerous journals, literary magazines, and publications. Her work is currently being taught at several universities both in the U.S. and abroad. She has given readings of her work in several venues around the United States. Academic papers about Famà and her work have been presented at conferences in the USA and in Italy. In 2002 and 2005, Maria Famà received the Aniello Lauri Award for Creative Writing. In 2003, she was Editor's Choice of the Paterson Literary Review, was a finalist in the 1998 Allen Ginsberg Poetry Awards, and won the 1994 Dream Images Poetry Award. In 2006, she was awarded the Amy Tritsch Needle Award for Poetry.

As part of Allegro, a video production company, Maria Famà wrote and produced two poetry videos and a video documentary on writer, Jerre Mangione. In addition, Famà has read her work on National Public Radio, appeared on television, and is featured reading her poetry in the award winning documentary film, "Prisoners Among Us" and in the documentary on the late jazz bagpipe musician, Rufus Harley, "Pipes of Peace."

VIA Folios

*A refereed book series dedicated to Italian studies
and the culture of Italian Americans in North America*

ANTHONY VALERIO
*Toni Cade Bambara's
One Sicilian Night*
Vol. 44, Poetry, $10

EMANUEL CARNEVALI
Dennis Barone, Ed.
Furnished Rooms
Vol. 43, Poetry, $14

BRENT ADKINS, et. al., Eds.
Shifting Borders, Negotiating Places
Vol. 42, Proceedings, $18

GEORGE GUIDA
Low Italian
Vol. 41, Poetry, $11

GARDAPHÉ, GIORDANO,
& TAMBURRI
Introducing Italian Americana
Vol. 40, Italian American Studies, $10

DANIELA GIOSEFFI
*Blood Autumn /
Autunno di sangue*
Vol. 39, Poetry, $15 / $25

FRED MISURELLA
Lies to Live by
Vol. 38, Stories, $15

STEVEN BELLUSCIO
Constructing a Bibliography
Vol. 37, Italian Americana, $15

ANTHONY J. TAMBURRI, Ed.
Italian Cultural Studies 2002
Vol. 36, Essays, $18

BEA TUSIANI
con amore
Vol. 35, Memoir, $19

FLAVIA BRIZIO-SKOV, Ed.
*Reconstructing Societies
in the Aftermath of War*
Vol. 34, History, $30

TAMBURRI, et. al., Eds.
Italian Cultural Studies 2001
Vol. 33, Essays, $18

ELIZABETH G. MESSINA, Ed.
In Our Own Voices
Vol. 32, Italian American Studies, $25

STANISLAO G. PUGLIESE
Desperate Inscriptions
Vol. 31, History, $12

HOSTERT & TAMBURRI, Eds.
Screening Ethnicity
Vol. 30, Italian American Culture, $25

G. PARATI & B. LAWTON, Eds.
Italian Cultural Studies
Vol. 29, Essays, $18

HELEN BAROLINI
More Italian Hours
Vol. 28, Fiction, $16

FRANCO NASI, Ed.
Intorno alla Via Emilia
Vol. 27, Culture, $16

ARTHUR L. CLEMENTS
The Book of Madness & Love
Vol. 26, Poetry, $10

JOHN CASEY, et. al.
Imagining Humanity
Vol. 25, Interdisciplinary Studies, $18

ROBERT LIMA
Sardinia / Sardegna
Vol. 24, Poetry, $10

DANIELA GIOSEFFI
Going On
Vol. 23, Poetry, $10

ROSS TALARICO
The Journey Home
Vol. 22, Poetry, $12

EMANUEL DI PASQUALE
The Silver Lake Love Poems
Vol. 21, Poetry, $7

JOSEPH TUSIANI
Ethnicity
Vol. 20, Poetry, $12

JENNIFER LAGIER
Second Class Citizen
Vol. 19, Poetry, $8

FELIX STEFANILE
The Country of Absence
Vol. 18, Poetry, $9

PHILIP CANNISTRARO
Blackshirts
Vol. 17, History, $12

LUIGI RUSTICHELLI, Ed.
Seminario sul racconto
Vol. 16, Narrativa, $10

LEWIS TURCO
Shaking the Family Tree
Vol. 15, Poetry, $9

LUIGI RUSTICHELLI, Ed.
Seminario sulla drammaturgia
Vol. 14, Theater/Essays, $10

FRED GARDAPHÉ
Moustache Pete is Dead!
Long Live Moustache Pete!
Vol. 13, Oral Literature, $10

JONE GAILLARD CORSI
Il libretto d'autore, 1860–1930
Vol. 12, Criticism, $17

HELEN BAROLINI
Chiaroscuro: Essays of Identity
Vol. 11, Essays, $15

PICARAZZI & FEINSTEIN, Eds.
An African Harlequin in Milan
Vol. 10, Theater/Essays, $15

JOSEPH RICAPITO
Florentine Streets & Other Poems
Vol. 9, Poetry, $9

FRED MISURELLA
Short Time
Vol. 8, Novella, $7

NED CONDINI
Quartettsatz
Vol. 7, Poetry, $7

ANTHONY J. TAMBURRI, Ed.,
Fuori: Essays by Italian / American
Lesbians and Gays
Vol. 6, Essays, $10

ANTONIO GRAMSCI
P. Verdicchio, Trans. & Intro.
The Southern Question
Vol. 5, Social Criticism, $5

DANIELA GIOSEFFI
Word Wounds & Water Flowers
Vol. 4, Poetry, $8

WILEY FEINSTEIN
Humility's Deceit: Calvino Reading
Ariosto Reading Calvino
Vol. 3, Criticism, $10

PAOLO A. GIORDANO, Ed.
Joseph Tusiani: Poet, Translator,
Humanist
Vol. 2, Criticism, $25

ROBERT VISCUSI
Oration Upon the Most Recent
Death of Christopher Columbus
Vol. 1, Poetry, $3

Published by Bordighera, Inc., an independent, not-for-profit, 501(c)3 scholarly organization that has no legal affiliation to Queens College/CUNY, the John D. Calandra Italian American Institute, or the University of Florida.

Book design by Lisa Cicchetti